Whatever is True

Also by

STEPHANIE CARDEL

This Isn't Shakespeare

WHATEVER IS TRUE

Youth Bible Study/Devotional

STEPHANIE CARDEL

WordCrafts Press

Unless otherwise noted, all Scripture quotations are from The ESV® Bible (The Holy Bible, English Standard Version®), © 2001 by Crossway, a publishing ministry of Good News Publishers. Used by permission. All rights reserved.

Scripture quotations marked NIV are taken from The Holy Bible, New International Version® NIV® Copyright © 1973, 1978, 1984, 2011 by Biblica, Inc. Used with permission. All rights reserved worldwide.

Whatever is True
Copyright © 2025
Stephanie Cardel

ISBN: 978-1-967649-29-7

All rights reserved. No part of this book may be reproduced, stored in a retrieval system, or transmitted in any form or by any means—electronic, mechanical, photocopy, recording or otherwise—without the prior written permission of the publisher. The only exception is brief quotations for review purposes.

Published by WordCrafts Press
Cody, Wyoming 82414
www.wordcrafts.net

Memory Verse:

Finally, brothers, whatever is true, whatever is honorable, whatever is just, whatever is pure, whatever is lovely, whatever is commendable, if there is any excellence, if there is anything worthy of praise, think about these things.

~Philippians 4:8 ESV

Theme Song:

"Look What You've Done," by Tasha Layton

Contents

Introduction 1
Week One: The Truth about Identity 3
   Day One - What Am I? 4
   Day Two – Goals 11
   Day Three – God's Plan For Me 17
   Day Four – Identity Theft 23
   Day Five – Discussion Questions 29
Week Two: The Truth about Purity 31
   Day One – Purity in Every Aspect of Life 32
   Day Two – Sexual Purity 37
   Day Three – Boundaries 44
   Day Four – Stronger Together 49
   Day Five – Discussion Questions 55
Week Three: The Truth about Love 57
   Day One – Types of Love 58
   Day Two – Relationships 63
   Day Three – Marriage 68
   Day Four – What Now? 74
   Day Five – Discussion Questions 81
   About the Author 83

Introduction

Before you begin, let me give you some guidance. I have provided the Bible verses that I recommend for you to read in the ESV version. It's always helpful to read several different versions of a passage, as well as the commentary from a study Bible to get a deeper meaning from it. I encourage you to do that. There are several apps (blueletterbible.org, studybible.org) so you can do that on your phone.

I hope you will do this study with a friend or two. Days one through four can be done on your own, maybe during your devotional time. The personal questions and takeaways are to help you process. You can share them or not. Day Five is only discussion questions. You can go through them yourself ahead of time, but they are meant to be for group discussion to get the most out of the study.

The themes in this study/devotional are in my YA novel, *This Isn't Shakespeare*, but you don't have to read the book to get something out of the study. The main character loves Shakespeare and is always quoting him. As a tie-in, I've started each day's study with a Shakespeare quote.

May this help you grow in your relationship with Christ, so you can stand firm against the culture and glorify God in all you do.

With Love in Christ,
Stephanie

P. S. Many thanks to Elle Cardel and Ryan Hudson for their insight and discerning critique and WordCrafts Press for publishing this as a companion book to my novel.

Week One

The Truth about Identity

Day One - What Am I?

> *"We know what we are but know not what we may be."*
> –Ophelia in William Shakespeare's *Hamlet*

The future is unpredictable and full of possibilities, that is true. But do we know what we are? Are we living in that certainty? This world bombards us with very worldly ideas about who we are and what we are. When you are told from a young age that you can choose your identity and this identity will define every aspect of your life, you accept it as truth. In fact, today, if you deny that and speak biblical truth about identity, you may face consequences. But the fact is, Christians don't choose their identity. They find it in their relationship with Christ. We know what we are. We are in Christ. Let's look at what that means.

Read Genesis 1:26–28; 2:7.

> *Then God said, "Let us make man in our image, after our likeness. And let them have dominion over the fish of the sea and over the birds of the heavens and over the livestock and over all the earth and over every creeping thing that creeps on the earth." So God created man in his own image, in the image of God he created him; male and female he created them.*
>
> *And God blessed them. And God said to them, "Be fruitful and multiply and fill the earth and subdue it and have dominion over the fish of the sea and over the birds of the heavens and over every living thing that moves on the earth."*
> ~Genesis 1:26–28
>
> *…then the Lord God formed the man of dust from the ground*

and breathed into his nostrils the breath of life, and the man became a living creature.

~Genesis 2:7

First, we are made in His image and given the breath of life. This doesn't mean we look like Him. It means only humans have been given a spirit capable of having a conscience and other capacities, like the ability to create art, that set us apart from the animals. It also means humans are His representatives on Earth to have authority over creation. And we have the ability to reflect His character in the way we love, and show patience, kindness, forgiveness, and faithfulness.

Read Genesis 6:5–6; Romans 3:23; 1 John 1:5–7; 1 Timothy 1:15–16.

The Lord saw that the wickedness of man was great in the earth, and that every intention of the thoughts of his heart was only evil continually. And the Lord regretted that he had made man on the earth, and it grieved him to his heart.

~Genesis 6:5–6

…for all have sinned and fall short of the glory of God.

~Romans 3:23

This is the message we have heard from him and proclaim to you, that God is light, and in him is no darkness at all. If we say we have fellowship with him while we walk in darkness, we lie and do not practice the truth. But if we walk in the light, as he is in the light, we have fellowship with one another, and the blood of Jesus his Son cleanses us from all sin.

~1 John 1:5–7

The saying is trustworthy and deserving of full acceptance, that Christ Jesus came into the world to save sinners, of whom I am the foremost. But I received mercy for this reason, that in me, as the foremost, Jesus Christ might display his perfect

patience as an example to those who were to believe in him for eternal life.
~1 Timothy 1:15–16

We are sinners. From birth, every inclination of our hearts is selfish. We have to learn to share and take turns and have patience with others; it doesn't come naturally. We want to do what we want to do when we want to do it. Because of this sinful nature, we deserve punishment. We deserve hell. But God sent Jesus to pay the punishment for us, so we can go to heaven if we repent of our sin and believe in Christ.

When we do that, the Holy Spirit enters our hearts and opens our eyes to a freedom from the unrelenting desire to sin by giving us a thankful spirit that wants to please God, worship Him, and not grieve Him.

Read Galatians 2:20; 1 John 1:9–10; Psalm 103:11–12; Ephesians 2:1–10.

I have been crucified with Christ. It is no longer I who live, but Christ who lives in me. And the life I now live in the flesh I live by faith in the Son of God, who loved me and gave himself for me.
~Galatians 2:20

If we confess our sins, he is faithful and just to forgive us our sins and to cleanse us from all unrighteousness. If we say we have not sinned, we make him a liar, and his word is not in us.
~1 John 1:9–10

For as high as the heavens are above the earth,
    so great is his steadfast love toward those who fear him;
As far as the east is from the west,
    so far does he remove our transgressions from us.
~Psalm 103:11–12

And you were dead in the trespasses and sins in which you

once walked, following the course of this world, following the prince of the power of the air, the spirit that is now at work in the sons of disobedience—among whom we all once lived in the passions of our flesh, carrying out the desires of the body and the mind, and were by nature children of wrath, like the rest of mankind. But God, being rich in mercy, because of the great love with which he loved us, even when we were dead in our trespasses, made us alive together with Christ—by grace you have been saved—and raised us up with him and seated us with him in the heavenly places in Christ Jesus, so that in the coming ages he might show the immeasurable riches of his grace in kindness toward us in Christ Jesus. For by grace you have been saved through faith. And this is not your own doing; it is the gift of God, not a result of works, so that no one may boast. For we are his workmanship, created in Christ Jesus for good works, which God prepared beforehand, that we should walk in them.

~Ephesians 2:1–10

We are forgiven. Our nature is to sin, and guilt can crush our spirit. But we don't have to live in guilt and shame. We just have to confess our sin and repent of it. The punishment for it all falls on Christ instead. We can have peace knowing our sins have been cast to the depths of the sea. The crushing weight of guilt is lifted from us. We are granted grace and mercy and given a thankful spirit. That spirit of thankfulness should shape every part of who we are and how we live.

Read 1 John 3:1–3; Ephesians 1:11–14, 2:19–22; Philippians 3:17–22.

See what kind of love the Father has given to us, that we should be called children of God; and so we are. The reason why the world does not know us is that it did not know him. Beloved, we are God's children now, and what we will be has not yet appeared; but we know that when he appears we shall be like him, because we shall see him as he is. And everyone who thus hopes in him purifies himself as he is pure.

~1 John 3:1–3

In him we have obtained an inheritance, having been predestined according to the purpose of him who works all things according to the counsel of his will, so that we who were the first to hope in Christ might be to the praise of his glory. In him you also, when you heard the word of truth, the gospel of your salvation, and believed in him, were sealed with the promised Holy Spirit, who is the guarantee of our inheritance until we acquire possession of it, to the praise of his glory.

~Ephesians 1:11–14

So then you are no longer strangers and aliens, but you are fellow citizens with the saints and members of the household of God, built on the foundation of the apostles and prophets, Christ Jesus himself being the cornerstone, in whom the whole structure, being joined together, grows into a holy temple in the Lord. In him you also are being built together into a dwelling place for God by the Spirit.

~Ephesians 2:19–22

Brothers, join in imitating me, and keep your eyes on those who walk according to the example you have in us. For many, of whom I have often told you and now tell you even with tears, walk as enemies of the cross of Christ. Their end is destruction, their god is their belly, and they glory in their shame, with minds set on earthly things. But our citizenship is in heaven, and from it we await a Savior, the Lord Jesus Christ, who will transform our lowly body to be like his glorious body, by the power that enables him even to subject all things to himself.

~Philippians 3:17–22

We are loved by God and heirs with Christ. With the certainty of God's love and the fellowship and community with other believers, our identity in Christ gives us stability in an unstable world, and dignity and courage in a world that is hostile and demeaning. It keeps us grounded, knowing this world is not our home. We are citizens of heaven and soldiers in God's army—fully armored for the battles we must fight and wounds we must endure. That doesn't mean we will always *feel* courageous. More often than not, we are fearful. But as we grow in faith and take hold of these truths, we most certainly will know who we are, what we are, and whose we are and will remember the armor He has graciously given to us.

Personal Questions:

Who are you?

What ways can you make your identity in Christ more foundational to all aspects of your life?

What are your takeaways from today's study?

Pray:

Lord, I know I'm a sinner undeserving of your mercy. Thank you for sending Jesus to live the life I can't live and take the punishment I deserve, so that I can come before you now and repent. Forgive me for so often letting the world shape my identity, for caving to peer pressure, for giving in to vanity. Let me be a light for You to the unsaved. Help me to fix my eyes on You instead of myself or this world, so that all aspects of my life are built on Christ, my Rock. Amen.

Day Two – Goals

"It is not in the stars to hold our destiny, but in ourselves."
—Cassius in William Shakespeare's *Julius Caesar.*

This quote means that we have choices about our destinies, our futures. We aren't puppets to fate, or astrology, or other people. We have agency. God has given us the freedom to choose. Now that we know our identity is in our relationship with Christ, how does that inform our choices about our future? If we live grounded in that truth, then instead of every inclination of our heart set on selfishness and sin, we have hearts full of thankfulness that want to glorify God with our actions.

Read Proverbs 3:5–12; 2 Timothy 2:14–16; Colossians 2:6–7.

Trust in the Lord with all your heart,
　and do not lean on your own understanding.
In all your ways acknowledge him,
　and he will make straight your paths.
Be not wise in your own eyes;
　fear the Lord, and turn away from evil.
It will be healing to your flesh
　and refreshment to your bones.
Honor the Lord with your wealth
　and with the firstfruits of all your produce;
then your barns will be filled with plenty,
　and your vats will be bursting with wine.
My son, do not despise the Lord's discipline
　or be weary of his reproof,
for the Lord reproves him whom he loves,

as a father the son in whom he delights.
~Proverbs 3:5–12

Remind them of these things and charge them before God not to quarrel about words, which does no good, but only ruins the hearers. Do your best to present yourself to God as one approved, a worker who has no need to be ashamed, rightly handling the word of truth. But avoid irreverent babble, for it will lead people into more and more ungodliness.
~2 Timothy 2:14–16

Therefore, as you received Christ Jesus the Lord, so walk in him, rooted and built up in him and established in the faith, just as you were taught, abounding in thanksgiving.
~Colossians 2:6–7

It's not necessary to ask God for a sign. He has told us what we should do when we need to make a decision. Scripture repeatedly tells us that to make a wise decision we should ask ourselves, "Will this path allow me to continue to glorify God, or will it lead me to sin?"

For example, if you're trying to decide what career you want to pursue. There are so many possibilities. You don't have to be in ministry to glorify God. You can be a light wherever you are. Seek out people in the jobs that interest you and ask them questions, maybe even shadow them for a day. There are lots of open doors. Many times, it's a choice between cake or pie. I mean, they're both good choices. Whatever choice you make *is* the choice God wants you to make. *Unless* you choose something that will cause you to sin.

So you should examine your motives to be wise in your choices. Do I just want to have that job for the money, the prestige, the good-looking co-worker, to prove something, to be able to boss people around…? God loves you and wants you to be happy, but our happiness in this world is just icing on the cake. Our true joy should always be in our relationship with Him. You don't have to stress over a decision when you think of it that way.

Does that mean the choice you make will always "prosper and not harm" you, as it says in Jeremiah 29:11? No. We can't expect to suddenly be transported to the world before the Fall where there was no sin, no darkness, no sickness. Life is difficult even when we make good choices with hearts that want to glorify God.

Read John 16:33; James 1:2–8.

> *I have said these things to you, that in me you may have peace. In the world you will have tribulation. But take heart; I have overcome the world.*
>
> ~John 16:33

> *Count it all joy, my brothers, when you meet trials of various kinds, for you know that the testing of your faith produces steadfastness. And let steadfastness have its full effect, that you may be perfect and complete, lacking in nothing.*
>
> *If any of you lacks wisdom, let him ask God, who gives generously to all without reproach, and it will be given him. But let him ask in faith, with no doubting, for the one who doubts is like a wave of the sea that is driven and tossed by the wind. For that person must not suppose that he will receive anything from the Lord; he is a double-minded man, unstable in all his ways.*
>
> ~James 1:2–8

It's all about our perspective in facing trials. We are called to remain faithful and thankful in all circumstances. This passage kind of makes it sound like God will give you whatever you ask for. But when it says "ask in faith" it means with a heart that seeks God's will. If what you ask for doesn't align with God's will for you then you won't get it. God is yesterday, today and tomorrow. He is not constrained by time. He knows if what we ask for is for our good or not.

Read 1 Samuel 24:1–22

> *When Saul returned from following the Philistines, he was*

told, "Behold, David is in the wilderness of Engedi." Then Saul took three thousand chosen men out of all Israel and went to seek David and his men in front of the Wildgoats' Rocks. And he came to the sheepfolds by the way, where there was a cave, and Saul went in to relieve himself. Now David and his men were sitting in the innermost parts of the cave. And the men of David said to him, "Here is the day of which the Lord said to you, 'Behold, I will give your enemy into your hand, and you shall do to him as it shall seem good to you.'" Then David arose and stealthily cut off a corner of Saul's robe. And afterward David's heart struck him, because he had cut off a corner of Saul's robe. He said to his men, "The Lord forbid that I should do this thing to my lord, the Lord's anointed, to put out my hand against him, seeing he is the Lord's anointed." So David persuaded his men with these words and did not permit them to attack Saul. And Saul rose up and left the cave and went on his way.

Afterward David also arose and went out of the cave, and called after Saul, "My lord the king!" And when Saul looked behind him, David bowed with his face to the earth and paid homage. And David said to Saul, "Why do you listen to the words of men who say, 'Behold, David seeks your harm'? Behold, this day your eyes have seen how the Lord gave you today into my hand in the cave. And some told me to kill you, but I spared you. I said, 'I will not put out my hand against my lord, for he is the Lord's anointed.' See, my father, see the corner of your robe in my hand. For by the fact that I cut off the corner of your robe and did not kill you, you may know and see that there is no wrong or treason in my hands. I have not sinned against you, though you hunt my life to take it. May the Lord judge between me and you, may the Lord avenge me against you, but my hand shall not be against you. As the proverb of the ancients says, 'Out of the wicked comes wickedness.' But my hand shall not be against you. After whom has the king of Israel come out? After whom do you pursue? After a dead dog! After a flea!

May the Lord therefore be judge and give sentence between me and you and see to it and plead my cause and deliver me from your hand."

As soon as David had finished speaking these words to Saul, Saul said, "Is this your voice, my son David?" And Saul lifted up his voice and wept. He said to David, "You are more righteous than I, for you have repaid me good, whereas I have repaid you evil. And you have declared this day how you have dealt well with me, in that you did not kill me when the Lord put me into your hands. For if a man finds his enemy, will he let him go away safe? So may the Lord reward you with good for what you have done to me this day. And now, behold, I know that you shall surely be king, and that the kingdom of Israel shall be established in your hand. Swear to me therefore by the Lord that you will not cut off my offspring after me, and that you will not destroy my name out of my father's house." And David swore this to Saul. Then Saul went home, but David and his men went up to the stronghold.

~1 Samuel 24:1–22

David is not always virtuous. In this passage, he starts down the wrong path. But then, he stops and listens to the Holy Spirit. He asks himself, "Am I doing this to glorify me or God?" Glorifying ourselves is ultimately the reason we sin. When we lose our temper, or don't do something we know we should, or do something we know we shouldn't, who gets the glory?

So many things can hijack us—even when we're on the right path. Life goals like our career, adventures we want to take, marriage, having children are all good and given by God for us to enjoy in this life. But we can't put them before God in our hearts. We have to remember that they are icing. God is the cake.

It's a good thing to set goals for yourself. It helps you have focus and motivation and to use your God-given gifts for their intended purpose. Setting goals with a Godly perspective keeps you from getting hijacked on the path to achieve them.

Personal Questions:

What are some goals you have for the future?

What are some ways you can glorify God as you accomplish your goals?

What are your takeaways from today's study:

Pray:

Heavenly Father, help me not to lean on my own understanding. Help me to stay in the Word and to pray regularly, so that I can hear your Holy Spirit. Forgive me when I seek to glorify myself instead of You. Give me a heart that longs to glorify You in all that I do. Amen.

Day Three - God's Plan For Me

> *"There are more things in heaven and earth, Horatio, than are dreamt of in your philosophy."*
> —Hamlet in William Shakespeare's *Hamlet.*

It can be overwhelming to apply the truths we discussed in day one and two. In this Shakespeare quote, Hamlet is telling Horatio that God's world is so vast and complex that we really understand very little of it. We'll never fully grasp concepts like the Holy Trinity or even how much God loves us on this side of heaven. But Scripture is our guide.

Read 2 Timothy 3:14–17; Acts 20:27; Psalm 33:11.

> *But as for you, continue in what you have learned and have firmly believed, knowing from whom you learned it and how from childhood you have been acquainted with the sacred writings, which are able to make you wise for salvation through faith in Christ Jesus. All Scripture is breathed out by God and profitable for teaching, for reproof, for correction, and for training in righteousness, that the man of God may be complete, equipped for every good work.*
> ~2 Timothy 3:14–17

> *…for I did not shrink from declaring to you the whole counsel of God.*
> ~Acts 20:27

> *The counsel of the Lord stands forever,*
>   *the plans of his heart to all generations*
> ~Psalm 33:11

Scripture is the whole revelation of God. From start to finish it points to Jesus. In the Old Testament it may be harder to see, but it is full of parallels, prophecy, types and shadows all pointing to WHO Jesus is, and WHAT He will do.

Read Ephesians 1:3–4; Romans 8:26–30.

> *Blessed be the God and Father of our Lord Jesus Christ, who has blessed us in Christ with every spiritual blessing in the heavenly places, even as he chose us in him before the foundation of the world, that we should be holy and blameless before him.*
> ~Ephesians 1:3–4

> *Likewise, the Spirit helps us in our weakness. For we do not know what to pray for as we ought, but the Spirit himself intercedes for us with groanings too deep for words. And he who searches hearts knows what is the mind of the Spirit, because the Spirit intercedes for the saints according to the will of God. And we know that for those who love God all things work together for good, for those who are called according to his purpose. For those whom he foreknew he also predestined to be conformed to the image of his Son, in order that he might be the firstborn among many brothers. And those whom he predestined he also called, and those whom he called he also justified, and those whom he justified he also glorified.*
> ~Romans 8:26–30

This means that everything that happens to you is part of God's plan for you—good and bad. (Although, there is human responsibility because we have free will and sometimes bad things happen as a consequence of our sin or the sin of someone else.) Some might think that God doesn't love them if He lets bad things happen to them. When we read a verse like Romans 8:28 that tells us "all things work together for good for those who are called according to His purpose," we might doubt it when bad things happen. But this "good" that God is working together is not us having earthly comfort. It's a greater "good." It's God's plan.

Read 2 Corinthians 3:16–18, 4:16–18, 5:17–21.

> *But when one turns to the Lord, the veil is removed. Now the Lord is the Spirit, and where the Spirit of the Lord is, there is freedom. And we all, with unveiled faces, beholding the glory of the Lord, are being transformed into the same image from one degree of glory to another. For this comes from the Lord who is the Spirit.*
>
> ~2 Corinthians 3:16–18

> *So we do not lose heart. Though our outer self is wasting away, our inner self is being renewed day by day. For this light momentary affliction is preparing for us an eternal weight of glory beyond all comparison, as we look not to the things that are seen but to the things that are unseen. For the things that are seen are transient, but the things that are unseen are eternal.*
>
> ~2 Corinthians 4:16–18

> *Therefore, if anyone is in Christ, he is a new creation. The old has passed away; behold, the new has come. All this is from God, who through Christ reconciled us to himself and gave us the ministry of reconciliation; that is, in Christ God was reconciling the world to himself, not counting their trespasses against them, and entrusting to us the message of reconciliation. Therefore, we are ambassadors for Christ, God making his appeal through us. We implore you on behalf of Christ, be reconciled to God. For our sake he made him to be sin who knew no sin, so that in him we might become the righteousness of God.*
>
> ~2 Corinthians 5:17–21

As believers we are gifted not only with understanding what

Christ has done for us, but by His grace and mercy, we are being transformed (through sanctification) into the image of Christ. Now in part, and at His second coming in full. We are new creations. Like butterflies still in the chrysalis, God is chipping away at our sin nature, transforming us. The trials we endure are a part of that. And instead of getting angry at God or blaming Him, we are called to be thankful in all circumstances, taking comfort in God's sovereignty to somehow work it all for good. We may never see HOW that happens on this side of heaven, so we are called to trust Him through it. I know it's hard to trust when I'm hurting. That's why staying rooted in my identity in Christ and the joy of my salvation, even in those valleys, is so important.

Read Phil. 2:12–18; 1 John 3:1–3

> *Therefore, my beloved, as you have always obeyed, so now, not only as in my presence but much more in my absence, work out your own salvation with fear and trembling, for it is God who works in you, both to will and to work for his good pleasure.*
>
> *Do all things without grumbling or disputing, that you may be blameless and innocent, children of God without blemish in the midst of a crooked and twisted generation, among whom you shine as lights in the world, holding fast to the word of life, so that in the day of Christ I may be proud that I did not run in vain or labor in vain. Even if I am to be poured out as a drink offering upon the sacrificial offering of your faith, I am glad and rejoice with you all. Likewise, you also should be glad and rejoice with me.*
>
> ~Philippians 2:12–18

> *See what kind of love the Father has given to us, that we should be called children of God; and so we are. The reason why the world does not know us is that it did not know him. Beloved, we are God's children now, and what we will be has not yet appeared; but we know that when he appears we shall be like him, because we shall see him as he is. And*

everyone who thus hopes in him purifies himself as he is pure.
~1 John 3:1–3

From all eternity that is God's plan for us.

Personal Questions:

How does it make you feel to consider that everything that happens—good and bad—is part of God's plan?

Can you think back on a difficult time and see God's hand in it? Maybe by the people He brought in your life (or removed from your life), the change in your heart, the goals He placed in your heart as a result, the empathy it gave you for others in that situation now?

What are your key takeaways from today's study?

Pray:

Sweet Jesus, there is so much sin and suffering in our lives. Help me take comfort from knowing that, somehow, it's all part of Your plan, and we are held by You. You will never leave us or forsake us. Our salvation is eternal. Help me look not to this world for comfort, but to You and your promise of eternal life. Help me to not lose heart, but to trust. Forgive my self-righteousness in the times I get angry with You. Thank you for being Merciful and Sovereign and Good all the time. Amen.

Day Four – Identity Theft

> "This above all: to thine own self be true, And it must follow, as the night the day, Thou canst not then be false to any man."
> —Polonius in William Shakespeare's *Hamlet*

Identity theft happens when someone steals your information, like credit card numbers, social security numbers, even just your name and birthdate. Sometimes it's photos or videos too. Then they impersonate you online and buy things or open new credit accounts all for fraudulent purposes. Although it's certainly a problem, and you should be extremely cautious with your online information, I want to explain a different kind of identity "theft."

I'm not sure if you're familiar with the story of Tom Sawyer painting Aunt Polly's fence, so bear with me as I recount it. It was a punishment, and Tom didn't want to do it. Tom was a clever boy, and he came up with a plan to get out of it. When some of his friends came along and started to tease him about having to work, Tom pretended that painting the fence was the most fun he'd ever had, and only he could be entrusted with this amazing job. He built it up so much that his friends begged him to let them try. He refused to the point that they bribed him with gifts to let them paint. So, for allowing them the privilege of having a turn painting, Tom received a kite, a one-eyed kitten, and some firecrackers. The fence was painted, and Tom barely did any of the work.

The culture we live in today does a similar trick. The media, the ads, the influencers are constantly telling us we aren't enough. We're too fat, or our hair isn't silky, or our clothes aren't stylish, or our skin isn't smooth. And if we only had (fill in the blank) it would be enough, we would be enough. Just like Tom, they're manipulating us, and we don't even realize it. We hear these messages so often that we believe them. Do you think Tom's friends admitted that painting the fence was NOT the most fun they ever had after they had paid for the privilege? Do you think we admit—even to ourselves—that we worry about not being enough?

This is why we must stay in the Word. We must pray daily. We must remember the truth of who we are and Whose we are. This culture is trying to steal our identity by convincing us that we aren't worth anything without what they can give us.

Read Isaiah 5:20–21, Colossians 2:6–10, Ephesians 6:10–20.

> *Woe to those who call evil good*
>   *and good evil,*
> *who put darkness for light*
>   *and light for darkness,*
> *who put bitter for sweet*
>   *and sweet for bitter!*
> *Woe to those who are wise in their own eyes,*
>   *and shrewd in their own sight!*
>   ~Isaiah 5:20–21

> *Therefore, as you received Christ Jesus the Lord, so walk in him, rooted and built up in him and established in the faith, just as you were taught, abounding in thanksgiving.*
> *See to it that no one takes you captive by philosophy and empty deceit, according to human tradition, according to the elemental spirits of the world, and not according to Christ. For in him the whole fullness of deity dwells bodily, and you have been filled in him, who is the head of all rule and authority.*
>   ~Colossians 2:6–10

> *Finally, be strong in the Lord and in the strength of his might. Put on the whole armor of God, that you may be able to stand against the schemes of the devil. For we do not wrestle against flesh and blood, but against the rulers, against*

> *the authorities, against the cosmic powers over this present darkness, against the spiritual forces of evil in the heavenly places. Therefore take up the whole armor of God, that you may be able to withstand in the evil day, and having done all, to stand firm. Stand therefore, having fastened on the belt of truth, and having put on the breastplate of righteousness, and, as shoes for your feet, having put on the readiness given by the gospel of peace. In all circumstances take up the shield of faith, with which you can extinguish all the flaming darts of the evil one; and take the helmet of salvation, and the sword of the Spirit, which is the word of God, praying at all times in the Spirit, with all prayer and supplication. To that end, keep alert with all perseverance, making supplication for all the saints, and also for me, that words may be given to me in opening my mouth boldly to proclaim the mystery of the gospel, for which I am an ambassador in chains, that I may declare it boldly, as I ought to speak.*
>
> ~Ephesians 6:10–20

If we don't fix our eyes on Jesus, abide in Him, and stand firm in the knowledge of who we are in Him, by Him, and through Him, we will be in danger of creating an identity for ourselves that is the opposite of what God is calling us to. We will listen to the world and believe our skin color, our sexual orientation, our nationality, our social class, or even our academic achievements are what define us. These things mean nothing before our God who only looks at the heart.

Read Matthew 6:19–21, 1 John 3:18–24

> *Do not lay up for yourselves treasures on earth, where moth and rust destroy and where thieves break in and steal, but lay up for yourselves treasures in heaven, where neither moth nor rust destroys and where thieves do not break in and steal. For where your treasure is, there your heart will be also.*
>
> ~Matthew 6:19–21

Little children, let us not love in word or talk but in deed and in truth.

By this we shall know that we are of the truth and reassure our heart before him; for whenever our heart condemns us, God is greater than our heart, and he knows everything. Beloved, if our heart does not condemn us, we have confidence before God; and whatever we ask we receive from him, because we keep his commandments and do what pleases him. And this is his commandment, that we believe in the name of his Son Jesus Christ and love one another, just as he has commanded us. Whoever keeps his commandments abides in God, and God in him. And by this we know that he abides in us, by the Spirit whom he has given us.

~1 John 3:18–24

Don't let the enemy steal your identity. The devil is much more manipulative than Tom Sawyer. He encourages us to sit on the fence, refusing to take a stand against sin for fear of what people will think. But we can't measure our worth by what people think, or what we accomplish, or what we own, or what we look like. The armor of God must be our identity protection. Pleasing God—not the world—must be our treasure.

Personal Questions:

Can you name a time that you were manipulated to do something you now regret?

Have you ever "sat on the fence" instead of choosing a side because of what people might think?

What are your takeaways from today's study?

Pray:

Oh Lord, thank you for giving me your Holy Spirit to guide me. Help me to abide in You so well that I can hear Your encouragement and keep a joyful heart. Forgive me for allowing myself to be manipulated by the world. Forgive me for the times I didn't stand up for You to be a light to others. Help me remember that Your opinion is the only one that matters. Amen.

THE TRUTH ABOUT IDENTITY IN PRACTICE

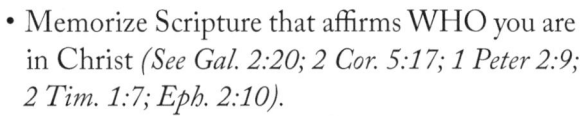

- Memorize Scripture that affirms WHO you are in Christ *(See Gal. 2:20; 2 Cor. 5:17; 1 Peter 2:9; 2 Tim. 1:7; Eph. 2:10).*
- Make time to read your Bible at least three times a week. *(Even better—join a Bible study.)*
- Set spiritual goals for yourself as well as life goals. *(Ex. Read one chapter of the Bible every day. Read one non-fiction spiritual encouragement book each year. Start a prayer journal.)*
- Before you get out of bed each morning spend time in prayer. *(Even short specific prayers like: Lord, guard my eyes and heart today; Holy Father, fill me with your Spirit; Heavenly Father, remind me of my worth in You when I'm tempted to seek it elsewhere.)*
- Examine your motives when you make a decision. *(Is this for your glory or God's?)*

Day Five - Discussion Questions

The culture tells us that we get to choose our identity. In light of this week's study, how would you argue against that idea?

Why is it not necessary to ask God for a sign?

What is God's will for you?

What can give us peace in the middle of hard circumstances?

Have you ever been disappointed after finally getting something you've been hoping for? Why didn't it live up to your expectations?

Have you ever been angry at God? If so, did your feelings change when you looked back on the situation?

Name two things you can do daily to help you remember WHO you are and WHOSE you are.

Week Two

The Truth about Purity

Day One – Purity in Every Aspect of Life

"The silence often of pure innocence persuades when speaking fails."
—Paulina in William Shakespeare's *The Winter's Tale.*

We've been looking at how our identity is in Christ, and what it looks like to live that out. When we start from that foundation, we are a new creation (2 Cor. 5:17). No longer is *every* inclination of our heart to sin (Gen. 6:5), because the Holy Spirit is guiding us, transforming us, giving us a desire to glorify God instead. We will stumble. We will take our eyes off Jesus, and like Peter we'll sink into the crashing waves (Matthew 14:22–33). Those waves represent the world, its busyness and its lies.

When we fix our eyes on Jesus we shine light into the darkness of the world. Our words and actions point to Him. As Paulina says in the above Shakespeare quote (I'm paraphrasing): actions speak louder than words. The word *purity* has been given a bad rep with the Purity Culture movement that some call toxic. That's not what I'm talking about here. Purity isn't about checking boxes—it's about living in the freedom and joy that comes from knowing Christ and having a relationship with Him. It's the goodness of creation *not* misused. Think of it as a synonym for truth, honor, and excellence. It means as a child of God we are called to have purity of motives, purity of thought, purity in speech, purity in how we dress, what we watch, and what we read.

God doesn't call us to purity to hold us back. He calls us to purity because of His love for us. He wants us to experience an abundant joy-filled life. What you pour in is what pours out. You can't pour in darkness and give off light. You can't pour in lies and be grounded in Truth. If we want to glorify God in all we do, then guarding our hearts from contamination from the lies of the world and striving for a heart that longs for purity in all things is essential.

Read Proverbs 4:20–27; 1 Timothy 4:12; 2 Timothy 2:22.

> *My son, be attentive to my words;*
> *incline your ear to my sayings.*
> *Let them not escape from your sight;*
> *keep them within your heart.*
> *For they are life to those who find them,*
> *and healing to all their flesh.*
> *Keep your heart with all vigilance,*
> *for from it flow the springs of life.*
> *Put away from you crooked speech,*
> *and put devious talk far from you.*
> *Let your eyes look directly forward,*
> *and your gaze be straight before you.*
> *Ponder the path of your feet;*
> *then all your ways will be sure.*
> *Do not swerve to the right or to the left;*
> *turn your foot away from evil.*
> ~Proverbs 4:20–27

> *Let no one despise you for your youth, but set the believers an example in speech, in conduct, in love, in faith, in purity.*
> ~1 Timothy 4:12

> *So flee youthful passions and pursue righteousness, faith, love, and peace, along with those who call on the Lord from a pure heart.*
> ~2 Timothy 2:22

In the NIV translation, Proverbs 4:23 says, *Above all else, guard your heart, for everything you do flows from it.* The Bible often refers to the heart as the center of our life and conscience and spirit. It is where the Holy Spirit "lives" in us. Guarding our heart with

Whatever is True

vigilance means listening to the Holy Spirit, filling up on good things, whatever is true, instead of the lies of the world.

Everything in God's creation is good. It's the misuse of these things that is sinful. For example, food is good. We need food. We enjoy food. But gluttony is a sin. When we indulge in gluttony, we are misusing food, giving in to those "youthful passions" Paul spoke of in the above verse. It's not the food that caused us to sin. That's why Paul tells Timothy to run away from youthful passions. He's saying, don't put yourself in a situation where you're tempted to give in to your desires and believe the lies of the world. Pursue the truth and stick with others who do that too.

Our culture blames those same "youthful passions" to excuse worldly behavior, but Paul says that's no excuse. God can use us no matter what our age to be an example to others and show them the Way. Purity is less about saying "no" to the world and more about saying a joyful "yes" to Jesus. When you love Him, you'll find yourself wanting to choose what honors Him.

Read Philippians 4:8–9; Psalm 51:10; Ephesians 4:29; Romans 12:1–2.

> *Finally, brothers, whatever is true, whatever is honorable, whatever is just, whatever is pure, whatever is lovely, whatever is commendable, if there is any excellence, if there is anything worthy of praise, think about these things. What you have learned and received and heard and seen in me—practice these things, and the God of peace will be with you.*
> ~Philippians 4:8–9

> *Create in me a clean heart, O God, and renew a right spirit within me.*
> ~Psalm 51:10

> *Let no corrupting talk come out of your mouths, but only such as is good for building up, as fits the occasion, that it may give grace to those who hear.*
> ~Ephesians 4:29

> *I appeal to you therefore, brothers, by the mercies of God, to present your bodies as a living sacrifice, holy and acceptable to God, which is your spiritual worship. Do not be conformed to this world, but be transformed by the renewal of your mind, that by testing you may discern what is the will of God, what is good and acceptable and perfect.*
>
> ~Romans 12:1–2

These verses sum up how we practically pursue a purity mindset. We are to pour in what is good. We are not supposed to be conformed to this world. We are not supposed to swear or talk about vulgar things. What kind of a witness for Christ are we if we use the f-bomb as an adjective, as so many do? A mindset of purity allows us to experience God's presence more fully and love Him more deeply because it keeps us rooted in the truth of His goodness and mercy.

Personal Questions:

Can you think of anything that you're doing that isn't "pure" and may be spilling into your heart?

Can you recall a stressful situation where you reacted with bitterness or profanity? Looking back, were you in a season where you'd been neglecting prayer and reading God's Word or surrounding yourself with people/books/movies/music that are filled with bitterness and swearing more than words of encouragement?

What is your key takeaway from today's study?

Pray:

Lord, I confess that I fill up on worldly things without giving thought to how it affects my heart, my witness, my actions. Forgive me and give me a desire to fill my heart with Your Word and other pure and righteous things, so that I will be a light for you in all situations and can live in the joy of your love. Amen.

Day Two – Sexual Purity

"Look thou be true; do not give dalliance too much rein. The strongest oaths are straw to the fire i' the blood."
—Prospero in *The Tempest* by William Shakespeare

Sex is a wonderful, sacred gift from God for married people to share. It's a good thing. It's meant to be enjoyed. It's the misuse of sex that is sinful. Sexual purity is God's plan for sex.

In the above quote, Prospero in *The Tempest* is warning his daughter's boyfriend, Ferdinand, to be true to his daughter, Miranda. He's already made him promise to wait until they marry to have sex earlier in the scene. Here he reminds him. *Do not give dalliance too much rein. The strongest oaths are straw to the fire i' the blood.* (Be careful. It's hard to keep a promise to abstain before marriage if you let your desires "have too much rein.") The question I so often get: How much is too much? How far can we go without crossing the line into "sin"?

The problem with pushing the limits with sexual activity is that once you've crossed a line, it doesn't seem like a big deal to cross it again. It's easy. In fact, it's hard to stop *before* that point. Which leads to crossing another line. And all sexual sin is a result of giving in to lust. Lust is sin, too. If you're doing everything else except actual intercourse so you can say you're still a virgin, you're missing the point. You aren't treating sex with the proper reverence it should have.

If you've already crossed lines you regret, hear this: in Christ, there is forgiveness, renewal, and a fresh start. Purity isn't about perfection in your past—it's about walking with Him today. "There is therefore now no condemnation for those who are in Christ Jesus," (Romans 8:1).

Read Galatians 5:16–17, 24; James 1:14–15.

But I say, walk by the Spirit, and you will not gratify the desires of the flesh. For the desires of the flesh are against the Spirit, and the desires of the Spirit are against the flesh, for these are opposed to each other, to keep you from doing the things you want to do… And those who belong to Christ Jesus have crucified the flesh with its passions and desires.
~Galatians 5:16–17, 24

But each person is tempted when he is lured and enticed by his own desire. Then desire when it has conceived gives birth to sin, and sin when it is fully grown brings forth death.
~James 1:14–15

Choosing sin creates distance between us and God, but when we turn to Him in repentance, He gives life, joy, and freedom we could never find anywhere else. When we listen to the lies of the world, we may start to believe sin isn't really sin and see no need to repent. Or maybe we deliberately sin because we think, I'll "repent" later. (Like the saying: ask forgiveness not permission.) That's not true repentance. God knows our hearts and our true motivations.

Some believe that the references to sexual sin in the New Testament are only speaking to those people in that time period in that particular culture. And that since Jesus said all we have to do is love God and love each other—and what could be more loving than sex?—the warnings don't apply. They *are* specific warnings for the people at that time, but they *do* apply to us too.

Read Matthew 22:34–40.

But when the Pharisees heard that he had silenced the Sadducees, they gathered together. And one of them, a lawyer, asked him a question to test him. "Teacher, which is the great commandment in the Law?" And he said to him, "You shall love the Lord your God with all your heart and with all your soul and with all your mind. This is the great and first

commandment. And a second is like it: You shall love your neighbor as yourself. On these two commandments depend all the Law and the Prophets."
~Matthew 22:34–40

On these two, depend ALL the Law and the Prophets. IF you were able to truly do that, you would be so aligned with the Spirit that you wouldn't sin at all. No human can do that fully this side of heaven. It's a summary of the ten commandments. It doesn't do away with them.

One of the commandments is don't commit adultery. What is the definition of adultery? Sex outside of marriage. Isn't premarital sex outside of marriage?

Read 1 Corinthians 6:9–20.

Or do you not know that the unrighteous will not inherit the kingdom of God? Do not be deceived: neither the sexually immoral, nor idolaters, nor adulterers, nor men who practice homosexuality, nor thieves, nor the greedy, nor drunkards, nor revilers, nor swindlers will inherit the kingdom of God. And such were some of you. But you were washed, you were sanctified, you were justified in the name of the Lord Jesus Christ and by the Spirit of our God.

"All things are lawful for me," but not all things are helpful. "All things are lawful for me," but I will not be dominated by anything. "Food is meant for the stomach and the stomach for food"—and God will destroy both one and the other. The body is not meant for sexual immorality, but for the Lord, and the Lord for the body. And God raised the Lord and will also raise us up by his power. Do you not know that your bodies are members of Christ? Shall I then take the members of Christ and make them members of a prostitute? Never! Or do you not know that he who is joined to a prostitute becomes one body with her? For, as it is written, "The two will become one flesh." But he who is joined to the Lord becomes one spirit with him. Flee from sexual

immorality. Every other sin a person commits is outside the body, but the sexually immoral person sins against his own body. Or do you not know that your body is a temple of the Holy Spirit within you, whom you have from God? You are not your own, for you were bought with a price. So glorify God in your body.

~1 Corinthians 6:9–20

The Corinthians were going along with the culture which encouraged them to satisfy all their desires, believing that didn't affect them spiritually. Paul is repeating some of the things they were saying like, "All things are lawful for me." So, there was a cultural component to all of Paul's admonishments pertaining to sexual sin, but that doesn't mean it doesn't apply to us today. Can we really say their culture was that different from ours? Maybe we don't have temple prostitutes, but we certainly have prostitution and pornography and all kinds of sexual sin.

Our main takeaway from Paul's admonishment to the Corinthians isn't "don't do this" and "don't do that." It's that he's saying there is a *spiritual* component to sex. We can't treat sex like eating—functional, enjoyable, but overall, not a big deal. He's saying it is a *very* big deal. It is sacred.

An argument I've heard before is that premarital sex isn't a sin if you love the person because you're treating it as something special and not casual. Scripture says otherwise.

Read Galatians 5:16–21; Ephesians 2:1–4; 1 John 2:15–17.

But I say, walk by the Spirit, and you will not gratify the desires of the flesh. For the desires of the flesh are against the Spirit, and the desires of the Spirit are against the flesh, for these are opposed to each other, to keep you from doing the things you want to do. But if you are led by the Spirit, you are not under the law. Now the works of the flesh are evident: sexual immorality, impurity, sensuality, idolatry, sorcery, enmity, strife, jealousy, fits of anger, rivalries, dissensions, divisions, envy, drunkenness, orgies, and things like these. I

warn you, as I warned you before, that those who do such things will not inherit the kingdom of God.
~Galatians 5:16–21

And you were dead in the trespasses and sins in which you once walked, following the course of this world, following the prince of the power of the air, the spirit that is now at work in the sons of disobedience—among whom we all once lived in the passions of our flesh, carrying out the desires of the body and the mind, and were by nature children of wrath, like the rest of mankind.
~Ephesians 2:1–4

Do not love the world or the things in the world. If anyone loves the world, the love of the Father is not in him. For all that is in the world—the desires of the flesh and the desires of the eyes and pride of life—is not from the Father but is from the world. And the world is passing away along with its desires, but whoever does the will of God abides forever.
~1 John 2:15–17

In the King James Version it says *fornication*, instead of sexual sin. Sexual sin can mean a lot of things, but fornication specifically means sex between two people who aren't married. Sexual sin includes fornication which by definition is premarital sex or adultery. So the argument that it's not sin if you love each other doesn't stand. There are no workarounds for sin. Giving in to your desires without the commitment inside the covenant of marriage or treating sex casually is letting Satan have a foothold in your newly transformed heart. Waiting for marriage is saying "yes" to God's best—His peace, His design for love, His joy.

Read Colossians 3:1–10.

If then you have been raised with Christ, seek the things that are above, where Christ is, seated at the right hand of God. Set your minds on things that are above, not on things that are on earth. For you have died, and your life is hidden with Christ in God. When Christ who is your life appears, then you also will appear with him in glory.

Put to death therefore what is earthly in you: sexual immorality, impurity, passion, evil desire, and covetousness, which is idolatry. On account of these the wrath of God is coming. In these you too once walked, when you were living in them. But now you must put them all away: anger, wrath, malice, slander, and obscene talk from your mouth. Do not lie to one another, seeing that you have put off the old self with its practices and have put on the new self, which is being renewed in knowledge after the image of its creator.
~Colossians 3:1–10

Love is wonderful. Desire is normal and healthy. Sexual chemistry is a good thing in a relationship bound for marriage—the only type of dating relationship worth having. But sex and all sexual activity is for marriage. God designed it as a gift to give each other not for self-serving purposes. *"But we're going to get married,"* you say. Well, then, it can wait. You can wait. Things happen. Sometimes plans change.

Look at it this way: have you changed much in the past three years? Do you want the person you were three years ago to make decisions for the person you are now? Three years isn't that long but think of all that's happened and what you've gone through. Three years from now you may be very different. You may want different things. You may have a different perspective on love and life.

Waiting for anything is difficult. Consider that waiting is a greater act of love than the physical intimacy you desire. You are saying to your future spouse that they were worth waiting for, that they are the only one you will trust completely with your whole self. That you value the sanctity of your marriage.

Personal Questions:

After today's study, are you rethinking the "how far is too far" question? What question should you ask instead?

Do you see how maintaining purity in all aspects of life (what you read, watch, listen to) can help you keep from engaging in sexual sin before marriage? Can you list any specific things in your life right now that aren't filling you with joy and peace?

What are your key takeaways from today's study?

Pray:

Heavenly Father, thank you for giving us love relationships. Help me to find completion in You and not other humans. Help me to put You first. Help me to guard my heart against sexual sin and give me strength to rein in my desires so that I can glorify You in all I do.

Day Three - Boundaries

"Every subject's duty is the king's, but every subject's soul is his own."
—King Henry in *Henry V* by William Shakespeare

If you play sports, you understand the importance of boundaries. All games must have rules. Our lives are somewhat bound by rules too. A civil society can't function without them. For example, how scary would it be to drive without speed limits, traffic signals, and stop signs? Sure, you know you would be careful, but who knows what someone else would do? Some people ignore the traffic laws already. Imagine if everyone did. Scary. Boundaries and laws are for our protection, not to control us.

We also need societal rules that are not laws but boundaries for behavior for our safety and to foster kindness. Like, don't talk with your mouth full; don't make fun of someone with a disability; don't forget to tell someone where you're going. These things have been taught to us our whole lives, so by this point, they're instinctual. We consider it just doing the right thing, not following rules.

Just like seatbelts don't take away your ability to enjoy a drive, God's boundaries don't take away joy. They keep you safe so you can experience life the way He designed it—abundant and good.

You've probably read these passages before, but this time read with the perspective of your identity in Christ and being a light to others.

Read 1 Corinthians 10:23; 1 Thessalonians 4:1–8; Hebrews 12:15–17; Psalm 19:13–14.

All things are lawful," but not all things are helpful. "All

things are lawful," but not all things build up.
~1 Corinthians 10:23

Finally, then, brothers, we ask and urge you in the Lord Jesus, that as you received from us how you ought to walk and to please God, just as you are doing, that you do so more and more. For you know what instructions we gave you through the Lord Jesus. For this is the will of God, your sanctification: that you abstain from sexual immorality; that each one of you know how to control his own body in holiness and honor, not in the passion of lust like the Gentiles who do not know God; that no one transgress and wrong his brother in this matter, because the Lord is an avenger in all these things, as we told you beforehand and solemnly warned you. For God has not called us for impurity, but in holiness. Therefore whoever disregards this, disregards not man but God, who gives his Holy Spirit to you.
~1 Thessalonians 4:1–8

See to it that no one fails to obtain the grace of God; that no "root of bitterness" springs up and causes trouble, and by it many become defiled; that no one is sexually immoral or unholy like Esau, who sold his birthright for a single meal. For you know that afterward, when he desired to inherit the blessing, he was rejected, for he found no chance to repent, though he sought it* with tears.
~Hebrews 12:15–17

*The blessing, not the repentance which he never sought.

Keep back your servant also from presumptuous sins;
  let them not have dominion over me!
Then I shall be blameless,
  and innocent of great transgression.
Let the words of my mouth and the meditation of my heart
  be acceptable in your sight,
  O Lord, my rock and my redeemer.
~Psalm 19:13–14

We are called to set boundaries so that we keep our feet on the right path. We need boundaries to pursue righteousness in all things—in what we read, watch, and do, where we go, and who we spend time with. We need boundaries in a love relationship, and boundaries with friends who are not on the right path and seek to pull us off it. Just like the rules of a game or the laws of society, boundaries are for our protection, another way we guard our heart from the lies of the world and live in abundant truth.

In today's Shakespeare quote, King Henry is saying the laws must be followed to keep us safe or for the safety of others. But keeping our soul safe isn't up to the government. It's up to us. We have to have a discerning Spirit. That means knowing our limits, setting boundaries, and seeking God's will.

Read 1 Peter 5:6–9; Psalm 119:101–104; Genesis 3:1–6.

Humble yourselves, therefore, under the mighty hand of God so that at the proper time he may exalt you, casting all your anxieties on him, because he cares for you. Be soberminded; be watchful. Your adversary the devil prowls around like a roaring lion, seeking someone to devour. Resist him, firm in your faith, knowing that the same kinds of suffering are being experienced by your brotherhood throughout the world.

~1 Peter 5:6–9

I hold back my feet from every evil way,
  in order to keep your word.
I do not turn aside from your rules,
  for you have taught me.
How sweet are your words to my taste,
  sweeter than honey to my mouth!
Through your precepts I get understanding;
  therefore I hate every false way.

~Psalm 119:101–104

Now the serpent was more crafty than any other beast of the field that the Lord God had made.

He said to the woman, "Did God actually say, 'You shall not eat of any tree in the garden'?" And the woman said to the serpent, "We may eat of the fruit of the trees in the garden, but God said, 'You shall not eat of the fruit of the tree that is in the midst of the garden, neither shall you touch it, lest you die.'" But the serpent said to the woman, "You will not surely die. For God knows that when you eat of it your eyes will be opened, and you will be like God, knowing good and evil." So when the woman saw that the tree was good for food, and that it was a delight to the eyes, and that the tree was to be desired to make one wise, she took of its fruit and ate, and she also gave some to her husband who was with her, and he ate.

~Genesis 3:1–6

The original sin was one of crossing a boundary. The world and Satan are still just as clever at convincing us that those boundaries aren't necessary, that we don't need to be "controlled." We're still falling for it. We're still looking for that workaround so we can do what we think *seems* right instead of listening to the Truth. Make no mistake. *Your adversary the devil prowls around like a roaring lion, seeking someone to devour,* and saying, *"You shall not surely die."* But there is sin and death and destruction at the end of that path. But inside the loving boundaries of our Father's arms, there is beauty, eternal life, joy, and peace. Boundaries are not oppressive. They are life-giving.

Personal Questions:

What are some boundaries you set for yourself?

Have you ever considered setting boundaries with friends? What types of boundaries could be beneficial in your friend relationships? (Ex. No gossiping, no letting them use foul language around you.)

What are your key takeaways from today's study?

Pray:

Lord, thank you for the boundaries you've given us. Help me to keep to the path You've set for me so that I may be a light for you. Give me the strength to set and keep boundaries in regard to purity in all aspects of my life. Guard my heart against the lies of the world. Amen.

Day Four - Stronger Together

> *"Those friends thou hast, and their adoption tried,*
> *Grapple them unto thy soul with hoops of steel…"*
> —Polonius in *Hamlet* by William Shakespeare

The Bible has much to say about the importance of true friends and even more about not being involved with false friends. In this Shakespeare quote, Polonius is advising his son before he leaves on a trip to hold tight to his trusted friends as if he were binding himself to them.

Read Ecclesiastes 4:9–12; Ephesians 4:11–16; Hebrews 10:23–25.

> *Two are better than one, because they have a good reward for their toil. For if they fall, one will lift up his fellow. But woe to him who is alone when he falls and has not another to lift him up! Again, if two lie together, they keep warm, but how can one keep warm alone? And though a man might prevail against one who is alone, two will withstand him—a threefold cord is not quickly broken.*
> ~Ecclesiastes 4:9–12

> *And he gave the apostles, the prophets, the evangelists, the shepherds and teachers, to equip the saints for the work of ministry, for building up the body of Christ, until we all attain to the unity of the faith and of the knowledge of the Son of God, to mature manhood, to the measure of the stature of the fullness of Christ, so that we may no longer be children, tossed to and fro by the waves and carried about by every*

wind of doctrine, by human cunning, by craftiness in deceitful schemes. Rather, speaking the truth in love, we are to grow up in every way into him who is the head, into Christ, from whom the whole body, joined and held together by every joint with which it is equipped, when each part is working properly, makes the body grow so that it builds itself up in love.
~Ephesians 4:11–16

Let us hold fast the confession of our hope without wavering, for he who promised is faithful. And let us consider how to stir up one another to love and good works, not neglecting to meet together, as is the habit of some, but encouraging one another, and all the more as you see the Day drawing near.
~Hebrews 10:23–25

Some people use the Ecclesiastes verses in their wedding ceremony. It is beautiful to show the symbolism of one cord as the husband, one as the wife, and one as Christ—a threefold cord. But it isn't specifically speaking about marriage in Ecclesiastes. It's saying in general, in life, if we have others to stand with us, we won't be easily defeated. We need other believers in our lives to encourage us, stand with us in the face of the world, and hold us accountable to stay on the right path.

Read Proverbs 13:20; Romans 15:5–7; 1 Thessalonians 5:9–11.

Whoever walks with the wise becomes wise, but the companion of fools will suffer harm.
~Proverbs 13:20

May the God of endurance and encouragement grant you to live in such harmony with one another, in accord with Christ Jesus, that together you may with one voice glorify the God and Father of our Lord Jesus Christ. Therefore welcome one another as Christ has welcomed you, for the glory of God.
~Romans 15:5–7

For God has not destined us for wrath, but to obtain salvation through our Lord Jesus Christ, who died for us so that whether we are awake or asleep we might live with him. Therefore encourage one another and build one another up, just as you are doing.

~1 Thessalonians 5:9–11

Not only do we need like-minded Christian friends, we also need mentors and other Godly people who can give us good advice. Our friends may be great at holding us accountable, but they may not be the best ones to ask for advice. If we aren't in youth group or bible study or attending church regularly so that we have options for people who are further along in their walk with the Lord than we are, it can be much more difficult to stay on right path. Don't assume that you can make an important decision on your own. Yes, you should pray about it. Yes, you should talk to your friends about it. But you need people who are older and wiser to help you, too. God gave us all different gifts so that everyone can build up the body of Christ, and we are stronger together.

Read 1 Corinthians 12:14–26.

For the body does not consist of one member but of many. If the foot should say, "Because I am not a hand, I do not belong to the body," that would not make it any less a part of the body. And if the ear should say, "Because I am not an eye, I do not belong to the body," that would not make it any less a part of the body. If the whole body were an eye, where would be the sense of hearing? If the whole body were an ear, where would be the sense of smell? But as it is, God arranged the members in the body, each one of them, as he chose. If all were a single member, where would the body be? As it is, there are many parts, yet one body.

The eye cannot say to the hand, "I have no need of you," nor again the head to the feet, "I have no need of you." On the contrary, the parts of the body that seem to be weaker are indispensable, and on those parts of the body that we think less honorable we bestow the greater honor, and our

unpresentable parts are treated with greater modesty, which our more presentable parts do not require. But God has so composed the body, giving greater honor to the part that lacked it, that there may be no division in the body, but that the members may have the same care for one another. If one member suffers, all suffer together; if one member is honored, all rejoice together.
~1 Corinthians 12:14–26

Jesus said, "…no city or house divided against itself will stand," (Matthew 12:25b).

Think about that. If you are double minded: living in sin, but claiming to love God, it can't stand. If you surround yourself with friends that aren't believers, constantly pulling you off the right path, it can't stand. If you don't fortify yourself by prayer and Bible study, and Christian friends who encourage you and call you out for sinful behavior and go to a church that preaches the truth and has mentors you can trust for Godly advice—you cannot stand. Remember what we read yesterday in 1 Peter: *…the devil prowls around like a roaring lion, seeking someone to devour.* You need the full armor of God and the community of other believers to stand against him.

Stronger together is part of a purity mindset. It's another way purity is not about saying "no" to sin but saying "yes" to abundant life. God doesn't call us to community only so we can be held accountable. It's so we can bear fruit for His glory. When we embrace this truth, it makes space for His Spirit to work through us in our own lives, in the lives of others, and in the church body.

Personal Questions:

How many people in your life are you able to truly be honest with about your struggles with sin? Have you asked them to hold you accountable? (Meaning, can you call them for encouragement to resist when you're tempted? Will they admonish you in private when they see you step out of line? Can you pray with them for encouragement when you slip up?)

Do you attend church regularly? If so, are there mentors there you can go to with your questions and struggles? List a few of them. If not, can you seek out a youth group or Bible study at a different church to find an encouraging environment? Ask some friends. Research online.

What is your key takeaway from today's study?

Pray:

Lord, I admit I need help. I am not strong enough to keep myself from worldly temptations. Please give me the courage to ask my friends to hold me accountable, to pray with me. Please help me find mentors that are Godly and speak Truth. Forgive me for giving in to the world so often. Give me a heart that longs to study Your Word and love and praise you all my life. Amen.

THE TRUTH ABOUT PURITY IN PRACTICE

- Memorize the theme verse Philippians 4:8 and consider all those things we are to "think about" an extension of the Way, the Truth, and the Life.
- Apply the concept of purity to every part of your life, what you say, what you watch, what you read, what you wear. Consider if it honors God and leads to peace and joy before you do it.
- Discuss the struggles you have with a trusted friend or mentor. Ask them to hold you accountable and do the same for them.
- Set boundaries seeking what glorifies God rather than yourself.
- Use your God-given gifts in some way within your church community.

Day Five - Discussion Questions

Have you ever considered purity to be important in all aspects of life and not just in regard to premarital sex? Did this week's study open your eyes to areas of your life that are lacking a purity mindset?

Are there decisions you have made in the past that you now regret? Have you ever considered that you might not like the decisions you make today three years from now? Does that affect how you want to be wise and seek Godly advice?

With how easily available pornography is today, what can you do to guard your heart and mind (and eyes) from it?

Is it a big deal to surround yourself with Christian friends? Do you think being a light to unbelievers means allowing yourself to enter into situations with them that you know are going to tempt you? How far is too far to go to maintain a friendship with an unbeliever? What can you do when opting out means feeling left out?

Do you think our pride sometimes causes us to think we can handle the Christian walk without support? Can you remember a situation where pride put you on the wrong path?

Week Three

The Truth about Love

Day One - Types of Love

"Doubt thou the stars are fire,
Doubt that the sun does move,
Doubt truth to be a liar,
But never doubt I love."
—from Hamlet's love letter to Ophelia
in *Hamlet* by William Shakespeare

You already know that there are lots of different kinds of love. We don't love pizza the same way we love our pets. But sometimes we love our pets the same way we love our siblings or other family. C.S. Lewis' book *The Four Loves* describes the main four types: Storge (store-gay)—affectionate/family love; Philia (feel-e-ah)—friendship love; Eros (Air-ohs)—romantic/sexual love; and Agape (Ah-gop-ay)—unconditional, selfless love/God's love.

We see examples of all the types of love in the Bible. Mary, Martha, and Lazarus showed familial love. David and Jonathan showed friendship love. The Song of Solomon speaks of romantic, physical love. And, of course, God's unconditional Agape love which encompasses all the types of love. It is perfect love.

Read John 15:13; Romans 5:7–8; 1 John 4:13–21.

Greater love has no one than this, that someone lay down his life for his friends.

~John 15:13

For one will scarcely die for a righteous person—though perhaps for a good person one would dare even to die— but God shows his love for us in that while we were still sinners,

Christ died for us.
~Romans 5:7–8

> *By this we know that we abide in him and he in us, because he has given us of his Spirit. And we have seen and testify that the Father has sent his Son to be the Savior of the world. Whoever confesses that Jesus is the Son of God, God abides in him, and he in God. So we have come to know and to believe the love that God has for us. God is love, and whoever abides in love abides in God, and God abides in him. By this is love perfected with us, so that we may have confidence for the day of judgment, because as he is so also are we in this world. There is no fear in love, but perfect love casts out fear. For fear has to do with punishment, and whoever fears has not been perfected in love. We love because he first loved us. If anyone says, "I love God," and hates his brother, he is a liar; for he who does not love his brother whom he has seen cannot love God whom he has not seen. And this commandment we have from him: whoever loves God must also love his brother.*
> ~1 John 4:13–21

We love because He first loved us. We are unable to experience real love without a relationship with God. His love for us = our transformed hearts = our salvation = our love for Him = our love for others. Our love for God is so transformative that it changes how we understand and experience love—all love. It changes how we view God's command to love others as He loves us.

Read 1 Corinthians 13.

> *If I speak in the tongues of men and of angels, but have not love, I am a noisy gong or a clanging cymbal. And if I have prophetic powers, and understand all mysteries and all knowledge, and if I have all faith, so as to remove mountains, but have not love, I am nothing. If I give away all I have, and if I deliver up my body to be burned, but have not love, I gain nothing.*

Whatever is True

Love is patient and kind; love does not envy or boast; it is not arrogant or rude. It does not insist on its own way; it is not irritable or resentful; it does not rejoice at wrongdoing, but rejoices with the truth. Love bears all things, believes all things, hopes all things, endures all things.

Love never ends. As for prophecies, they will pass away; as for tongues, they will cease; as for knowledge, it will pass away. For we know in part and we prophesy in part, but when the perfect comes, the partial will pass away. When I was a child, I spoke like a child, I thought like a child, I reasoned like a child. When I became a man, I gave up childish ways. For now we see in a mirror dimly, but then face to face. Now I know in part; then I shall know fully, even as I have been fully known.

So now faith, hope, and love abide, these three; but the greatest of these is love.

~1 Corinthians 13

We can't love others perfectly this side of heaven and our complete sanctification, but our relationship with God, our understanding of His Love for us allows us to have the greatest example of love. I'm not saying unbelievers can't experience love, but I do believe the love they experience is only an echo of what true love is. Because if it's difficult for us believers to be selfless and forgiving, and exhibit all the other attributes of love, how much more difficult is it for them who haven't experienced the transforming power of God's unconditional love? How can they truly forgive others when they haven't experienced God's undeserved forgiveness and mercy? Where is there hope? Where is their faith? These three abide: faith, hope, and love. That means these three are essential and lasting. And the greatest of these is love.

Read 1 Peter 4:8; Romans 13:8–10.

Above all, keep loving one another earnestly, since love covers a multitude of sins.

~1 Peter 4:8

> *Owe no one anything, except to love each other, for the one who loves another has fulfilled the law. For the commandments, "You shall not commit adultery, You shall not murder, You shall not steal, You shall not covet," and any other commandment, are summed up in this word: "You shall love your neighbor as yourself." Love does no wrong to a neighbor; therefore love is the fulfilling of the law.*
>
> ~Romans 13:8–10

Not only can we not experience true love without God's Agape love for us, but we also can't begin to live a life rejecting sin. Jesus said the commandments can be summed up into two commandments: love God with all your heart and love others as much as you love yourself. If we love God with all our heart, we won't have other gods, or take His name in vain, or neglect to rest and worship on the Sabbath. And if we love others well, we'll honor our parents, we won't commit murder or adultery or theft. We won't lie about others or covet their things either.

Obviously, we do sin. We do break commandments. But if we strive to love, truly love God and other people, it will be easier to glorify God in all we do and keep His commandments.

Personal Questions:

When you read the verse about no greater love than someone who lays down their life for a friend (John 15:13) what does it mean to you?

Have you ever been angry with someone and offered up forgiveness anyway? Have you held a grudge? Do you think it's biblical to hold a grudge? How does considering how much we've been forgiven help us to forgive?

What's your key takeaway from today's study?

Pray:

Heavenly Father, I pray you would help me love You and love others selflessly. I admit my own selfish desires and expectations cause me to be angry and sin against You and those I claim to love. Help me to remember how You have forgiven me even though I don't deserve it. Help me to remember that love is humble and kind and doesn't insist on its own way or get resentful. Help me to love like You love. Amen.

Day Two – Relationships

> "The course of true love never did run smooth."
> —Lysander in *A Midsummer's Night Dream*
> by William Shakespeare

*L*ove is great in all its forms, but love is hard. At our core we are selfish, and we have to fight that trait all the days of our lives. When we are openly showing love for someone, it's easy to be selfless. But the rest of the time—not so much.

Read Galatians 6:9–10; Philippians 2:1–8; James 3:16–18.

> *And let us not grow weary of doing good, for in due season we will reap, if we do not give up. So then, as we have opportunity, let us do good to everyone, and especially to those who are of the household of faith.*
> ~Galatians 6:9–10

> *So if there is any encouragement in Christ, any comfort from love, any participation in the Spirit, any affection and sympathy, complete my joy by being of the same mind, having the same love, being in full accord and of one mind. Do nothing from selfish ambition or conceit, but in humility count others more significant than yourselves. Let each of you look not only to his own interests, but also to the interests of others. Have this mind among yourselves, which is yours in Christ Jesus, who, though he was in the form of God, did not count equality with God a thing to be grasped, but emptied himself, by taking the form of a servant, being born in the likeness of men. And being found in human form, he humbled himself by*

becoming obedient to the point of death, even death on a cross.
~Philippians 2:1–8

For where jealousy and selfish ambition exist, there will be disorder and every vile practice. But the wisdom from above is first pure, then peaceable, gentle, open to reason, full of mercy and good fruits, impartial and sincere. And a harvest of righteousness is sown in peace by those who make peace.
~James 3:16–18

After those last verses, James goes on (in chapter four) to remind us that friendship with the world makes you an enemy of God. That's why it's so important that we identify as belonging to Christ and make our relationship with Him our priority. Remember, we only love because He first loved us. So, we must first love Him in order to love others well. In our family, in our friendships, in our romantic relationships we are often quick to be offended, quick to anger, and quick to speak an unkind word. We assume the worst intentions of others then get angry when they do the same regarding us. We use words like always and never far too much. (You always forget… You never help when…) Where are our hearts when we say these things? Focused on ourselves.

If we stopped to pray first, if we stopped to remember that we're guilty of doing the same things sometimes, if we even just gave the other person the benefit of the doubt instead of assuming the worst of their motives, how different would our reactions and interactions be? Wouldn't it be great if we were quick to forgive instead of quick to be resentful?

Read Colossians 3:12–17; Galatians 5:13–15; Ephesians 4:1–3; Proverbs 17:17.

Put on then, as God's chosen ones, holy and beloved, compassionate hearts, kindness, humility, meekness, and patience, bearing with one another and, if one has a complaint against another, forgiving each other; as the Lord has forgiven you, so you also must forgive. And above all these put on love, which

binds everything together in perfect harmony. And let the peace of Christ rule in your hearts, to which indeed you were called in one body. And be thankful. Let the word of Christ dwell in you richly, teaching and admonishing one another in all wisdom, singing psalms and hymns and spiritual songs, with thankfulness in your hearts to God. And whatever you do, in word or deed, do everything in the name of the Lord Jesus, giving thanks to God the Father through him.
~Colossians 3:12–17

For you were called to freedom, brothers. Only do not use your freedom as an opportunity for the flesh, but through love serve one another. For the whole law is fulfilled in one word: "You shall love your neighbor as yourself." But if you bite and devour one another, watch out that you are not consumed by one another.
~Galatians 5:13–15

I therefore, a prisoner for the Lord, urge you to walk in a manner worthy of the calling to which you have been called, with all humility and gentleness, with patience, bearing with one another in love, eager to maintain the unity of the Spirit in the bond of peace.
~Ephesians 4:1–3

*A friend loves at all times,
    and a brother is born for adversity.*
~Proverbs 17:17

Forgiveness is vital to the Christian in a relationship because resentment in our hearts is a weed that chokes out love. But we also have to guard our hearts against those who aren't repentant and continue in abusive behavior. Abuse can be obvious, such as physical harm or the mental abuse of cutting words. But sometimes it's more subtle. It can take the form of blaming others and not taking responsibility for actions. In other words, playing on our sympathies. They might also make you feel needed as they take and take and never reciprocate, leaving you empty physically and spiritually. Or maybe they use backhanded compliments that sound nice on the surface but have an underlying message meant to demean.

Christian forgiveness doesn't mean we are to lay down and take abuse, forgiving over and over, or assuming the best motives when actions prove the motives were not good. These are the times where we need discernment and the counsel of other Christians. Not everyone who claims to be a Christian has had their heart changed by the Holy Spirit. We are called not to "yoke" ourselves to unbelievers (2 Corinthians 6:14). This means we can be a light and point to Christ among unbelievers, but we should use caution in relationships with them where they may have influence over us, instead of the other way around.

We are going to have relationships with unbelievers—it's unavoidable. Just remember that showing kindness and giving forgiveness doesn't mean you can't call them out for abusive behavior and walk away from that relationship if they continue to hurt you or make you feel less than the amazing child of God you are.

Read Hebrews 10:24–25; Proverbs 27:17.

> *And let us consider how to stir up one another to love and good works, not neglecting to meet together, as is the habit of some, but encouraging one another, and all the more as you see the Day drawing near.*
> ~Hebrews 10:24–25

> *Iron sharpens iron,*
> *and one man sharpens another.*
> ~Proverbs 27:17

Choose who you have relationships with wisely. You want to have people around you that build you up and encourage you. Be iron that sharpens iron for each other.

Personal Questions:

When you have been angry with someone in the past, were you quick to assume they intended to hurt you? Looking back, could you have been wrong?

Do you have friendships that build you up? Are you also the kind of friend that encourages and supports?

What are your key takeaways from today's study?

Pray:

Heavenly Father, help me to be more discerning in my relationships. Guide me to love as You have loved, so I am not self-seeking and don't assume the worst in others' motives. But also help me to see when someone is taking advantage of me or really does have unkind motives. Surround me with those that will support and encourage me and give me the heart to be able to do the same for them. Help me to abide in You first and always. Amen.

Day Three - Marriage

Let me not to the marriage of true minds
Admit impediments; love is not love
Which alters when it alteration finds,
Or bends with the remover to remove.
O no, it is an ever-fixèd mark
That looks on tempests and is never shaken;
It is the star to every wand'ring bark
Whose worth's unknown, although his height be taken.
Love's not time's fool, though rosy lips and cheeks
Within his bending sickle's compass come.
Love alters not with his brief hours and weeks,
But bears it out even to the edge of doom:
If this be error and upon me proved,
I never writ, nor no man ever loved.
        —*Sonnet 116* by William Shakespeare

Shakespeare speaks a lot of truth. True love is not altered when you find out your spouse drools in their sleep or leaves their dirty socks on the floor. Loving someone enough to marry them means loving all of them—faults and all. Have you ever listened closely to marriage vows? Before God and witnesses they promise to love, honor, respect, faithfully commit through sickness, poverty, highs and lows, and to put the one they marry before every other human in their life until the day they die. That's a big deal. Marriage shouldn't be entered into lightly.

Read Genesis 2:24; Matthew 19:4–6.

Therefore a man shall leave his father and his mother and

hold fast to his wife, and they shall become one flesh.
~Genesis 2:24

He answered, "Have you not read that he who created them from the beginning made them male and female, and said, 'Therefore a man shall leave his father and his mother and hold fast to his wife, and the two shall become one flesh'? So they are no longer two but one flesh. What therefore God has joined together, let not man separate."
~Matthew 19:4–6

Most pastors require counseling before they will perform a marriage ceremony for the couple. As I have repeatedly said, we are naturally selfish. So how do people keep those vows? What the marriage vows don't mention is compromise. There will be a lot of compromise when you start living with someone. Especially if you didn't have siblings or have lived alone for a long time. We get set in our ways. It's a big adjustment.

Read Proverbs 3:3–4; 2 Peter 1:5–7; Ephesians 4:32.

Let not steadfast love and faithfulness forsake you;
 bind them around your neck;
 write them on the tablet of your heart.
So you will find favor and good success
 in the sight of God and man.
~Proverbs 3:3–4

For this very reason, make every effort to supplement your faith with virtue, and virtue with knowledge, and knowledge with self-control, and self-control with steadfastness, and steadfastness with godliness, and godliness with brotherly affection, and brotherly affection with love.
~2 Peter 1:5–7

Be kind to one another, tenderhearted, forgiving one another, as God in Christ forgave you.
~Ephesians 4:32

Some people get caught up in romance, and their imagination paints a rosy picture of a happily ever after that forgets about the boring routine of life like sharing a bathroom sink with someone. Or coming home tired from work and having to figure out something to eat for dinner for two people day after day. And what about dirty clothes? And dirty dishes? They pile up fast. Day-to-day life isn't romantic.

Read 1 Peter 4:8; Colossians 3:14; Ephesians 4:2

> *Above all, keep loving one another earnestly, since love covers a multitude of sins.*
>
> ~1 Peter 4:8

> *And above all these put on love, which binds everything together in perfect harmony.*
>
> ~Colossians 3:14

> *…with all humility and gentleness, with patience, bearing with one another in love…*
>
> ~Ephesians 4:2

That's why it's so important to choose the right person. I can't count how many times I've been asked, "How do you know if he or she is the one?" You pray for discernment. The Holy Spirit will give you a deep, abiding certainty. Make a list of the qualities you want in a future spouse? Does this person measure up? Then, ask yourself these questions: Do we have a great rapport? (In other words, do we "get" each other and share a similar sense of humor?) Is he or she the last person I want to talk to before I sleep, and the first person I want to see when I wake up? Do I even want to imagine a future *without* this person? Is he or she the first person I want to tell my good or bad news to? If this person were in an accident and became paralyzed so that they couldn't have sex or have children, would I still want to spend the rest of my life with her/him? Do I cherish this person?

Does this person cherish *me*?

Because it has to be reciprocal. Don't be blinded by your own feelings. If they aren't interested in marriage at all, or if they "love" you, but it's just friendship love, they are not the one God has for you. Even if it breaks your heart, you can't continue in a relationship with that person. God will honor your faithfulness to put Him first and will raise up the right person. Trust and pray.

Remember I told you: love is not easy. Marriage is even more difficult. It's sharing everything, every day, and being there for each other no matter what. It's arguing with respect and not letting your anger guide you.

Sometimes people get married for the wrong reasons. They're lonely. They're needy. They want to have sex. Those reasons are about their own needs. Don't get married for you. Get married to be the other half, the iron that sharpens iron of the one you marry.

It's not about what they can do for you. Even sex is not about you. In a true love relationship, it's about giving pleasure to the one you love. Your giving of pleasure should be its own reward when you love someone. Your receiving pleasure too, is a bonus.

God made sex as a gift. One of the reasons it's important to wait until you're married to have sex is that the brain gives off chemicals during sex that help us bond with that person. If you have sex with lots of different people before marriage (or if you watch/read porn and masturbate a lot) your brain gets confused and that doesn't happen. So, saving sex for marriage is not just about purity in all aspects of life in order to honor God and glorify Him in all you do. It's also another way to show love for your future spouse.

Read Song of Solomon 6:3a; Mark 10:9; Hebrews 13:4

I am my beloved's and my beloved is mine.
~Song of Solomon 6:3

What therefore God has joined together, let not man separate.
~Mark 10:9

Let marriage be held in honor among all, and let the

marriage bed be undefiled, for God will judge the sexually immoral and adulterous.

~Hebrews 13:4

Remember the threefold cord verse? Now you see why people use it in marriage ceremonies. Marriage is hard work, and if Christ is not first in your heart and your spouse's heart, you can't be iron, you can't put them first, and you don't want to. *Greater love has no one than this, that someone lay down his life for his friends* (John 15:13). That's Agape love, God's love. And the second greatest love is marriage love that strives to copy God's Agape love because it, too, has to encompass all the types of love.

Personal Questions:

Have you dated people before that you knew you would never marry? Why or why not?

Is there a couple in your life that exemplifies true love in their marriage? If not, it may be harder for you to learn to argue respectfully and put Christ first in your own relationships. Do you strive to do that in your friendships?

What are your key takeaways from today's study?

Pray:

Lord, I thank you for showing me what real love looks like. I pray you give me discernment when it comes time for me to marry. I lift up the person you have chosen for me and pray for his/her safety and purity. I ask that you give me a heart that longs to treat sex like the gift that it is so that I can remain pure for my future spouse. Amen.

Day Four – What Now?

> *That, in the course of justice, none of us*
> *Should see salvation: we do pray for mercy;*
> *And that same prayer doth teach us all to render*
> *The deeds of mercy.*
> —Portia in *The Merchant of Venice*
> by William Shakespeare

What does the Lord require of us? To act justly, to love mercy, and to walk humbly with our God (Micah 6:8). This Shakespeare quote speaks to that. Portia is saying it isn't just and fair for us to get to go to heaven. It's only because of God's mercy in sending Jesus to take the punishment for us. So in the same way mercy has been extended to us, we should be merciful to others.

With our identity firmly rooted in Christ alone, our minds set to pursue purity in all things, and love and mercy as our guiding principles, what is next? We can say it, but how do we live it? It sounds good. We believe it's good and want to do it but remember what Paul says in Romans.

Read Romans 7:15–8:17.

> *For I do not understand my own actions. For I do not do what I want, but I do the very thing I hate. Now if I do what I do not want, I agree with the law, that it is good. So now it is no longer I who do it, but sin that dwells within me. For I know that nothing good dwells in me, that is, in my flesh. For I have the desire to do what is right, but not the ability to carry it out. For I do not do the good I want, but the evil I do not want is what I keep on doing. Now if*

I do what I do not want, it is no longer I who do it, but sin that dwells within me.

So I find it to be a law that when I want to do right, evil lies close at hand. For I delight in the law of God, in my inner being, but I see in my members another law waging war against the law of my mind and making me captive to the law of sin that dwells in my members. Wretched man that I am! Who will deliver me from this body of death? Thanks be to God through Jesus Christ our Lord! So then, I myself serve the law of God with my mind, but with my flesh I serve the law of sin.

8 There is therefore now no condemnation for those who are in Christ Jesus. For the law of the Spirit of life has set you free in Christ Jesus from the law of sin and death. For God has done what the law, weakened by the flesh, could not do. By sending his own Son in the likeness of sinful flesh and for sin, he condemned sin in the flesh, in order that the righteous requirement of the law might be fulfilled in us, who walk not according to the flesh but according to the Spirit. For those who live according to the flesh set their minds on the things of the flesh, but those who live according to the Spirit set their minds on the things of the Spirit. For to set the mind on the flesh is death, but to set the mind on the Spirit is life and peace. For the mind that is set on the flesh is hostile to God, for it does not submit to God's law; indeed, it cannot. Those who are in the flesh cannot please God.

You, however, are not in the flesh but in the Spirit, if in fact the Spirit of God dwells in you. Anyone who does not have the Spirit of Christ does not belong to him. But if Christ is in you, although the body is dead because of sin, the Spirit is life because of righteousness. If the Spirit of him who raised Jesus from the dead dwells in you, he who raised Christ Jesus from the dead will also give life to your mortal bodies through his Spirit who dwells in you.

So then, brothers, we are debtors, not to the flesh, to live according to the flesh. For if you live according to the flesh

you will die, but if by the Spirit you put to death the deeds of the body, you will live. For all who are led by the Spirit of God are sons of God. For you did not receive the spirit of slavery to fall back into fear, but you have received the Spirit of adoption as sons, by whom we cry, "Abba! Father!" The Spirit himself bears witness with our spirit that we are children of God, and if children, then heirs—heirs of God and fellow heirs with Christ, provided we suffer with him in order that we may also be glorified with him.
~Romans 7:15–8:17

This is an encapsulation of the Gospel, and what it means to be living in the ongoing process of sanctification. Let me break it down for you. God gave us the law so we would have a model of right and wrong. But giving us the law didn't stop us from breaking the law because every inclination of our hearts is toward sin.

The law reveals that we deserve condemnation/judgment/punishment because we can't keep it. BUT GOD in his mercy sent Jesus to be an offering for our sin. (Like the OT blood sacrifices. Except we don't have to do it over and over because He was the one and only perfect sacrifice for all time.) Praise God! And now that the price is paid, if we repent and ask Jesus to come into our hearts, the Holy Spirit changes us, makes us new—a person no longer *ruled* by our sinful nature. We no longer want to live "by the flesh" because we understand how that grieves the LORD instead of glorifying Him.

That's when the sanctification process begins. (And He that began a good work in you, will bring it to completion—Philippians 1:6.) With the assurance of eternal life, the thankfulness we feel for His mercy, and the power of the Holy Spirit to call upon, we grow in confidence and peace. We fix our eyes on the Truth, anchor ourselves with it, continually reminding ourselves who we are in Christ. We seek to be honest and specific regarding our sin and repent daily. We feed our hearts, minds and souls with God's Word, and saturate ourselves in Its wisdom.

Read Ephesians 2:1–10; Colossians 3:1–17.

STEPHANIE CARDEL

And you were dead in the trespasses and sins in which you once walked, following the course of this world, following the prince of the power of the air, the spirit that is now at work in the sons of disobedience— among whom we all once lived in the passions of our flesh, carrying out the desires of the body and the mind, and were by nature children of wrath, like the rest of mankind. But God, being rich in mercy, because of the great love with which he loved us, even when we were dead in our trespasses, made us alive together with Christ—by grace you have been saved—and raised us up with him and seated us with him in the heavenly places in Christ Jesus, so that in the coming ages he might show the immeasurable riches of his grace in kindness toward us in Christ Jesus. For by grace you have been saved through faith. And this is not your own doing; it is the gift of God, not a result of works, so that no one may boast. For we are his workmanship, created in Christ Jesus for good works, which God prepared beforehand, that we should walk in them.
~Ephesians 2:1–10

If then you have been raised with Christ, seek the things that are above, where Christ is, seated at the right hand of God. Set your minds on things that are above, not on things that are on earth. For you have died, and your life is hidden with Christ in God. When Christ who is your life appears, then you also will appear with him in glory.

Put to death therefore what is earthly in you: sexual immorality, impurity, passion, evil desire, and covetousness, which is idolatry. On account of these the wrath of God is coming. In these you too once walked, when you were living in them. But now you must put them all away: anger, wrath, malice, slander, and obscene talk from your mouth. Do not lie to one another, seeing that you have put off the old self with its practices and have put on the new self, which is being renewed in knowledge after the image of its creator. Here there is not Greek and Jew, circumcised and uncircumcised,

barbarian, Scythian, slave, free; but Christ is all, and in all. Put on then, as God's chosen ones, holy and beloved, compassionate hearts, kindness, humility, meekness, and patience, bearing with one another and, if one has a complaint against another, forgiving each other; as the Lord has forgiven you, so you also must forgive. And above all these put on love, which binds everything together in perfect harmony. And let the peace of Christ rule in your hearts, to which indeed you were called in one body. And be thankful. Let the word of Christ dwell in you richly, teaching and admonishing one another in all wisdom, singing psalms and hymns and spiritual songs, with thankfulness in your hearts to God. And whatever you do, in word or deed, do everything in the name of the Lord Jesus, giving thanks to God the Father through him.
~Colossians 3:1–17

What else can we do? We set our minds on things that are "above," putting to death what is worldly in us. We put on kindness, humility, meekness, patience, and above all LOVE. We stay thankful for everything and let that thankfulness give us joy and peace in the face of sorrow and anxiety.

That is HOW we live in this world that has become so dark. That is HOW we shine and glorify God in all we do.

Personal Questions

List a few specific things you can start doing today that will help you live a life led by the Spirit.

If you haven't believed in Jesus Christ as your savior yet, pray this prayer:

In Jesus name, I ask you to open my eyes to the truth. Lord, I acknowledge that I am a sinner in thought, word, and deed. Please forgive me. I know I can't turn from my sin without your help, and I know I deserve punishment and eternal death for my sin. Thank you for sending Jesus. I believe He paid for all my sins with his death on the cross, so that I can be forgiven and have eternal life. Send your Holy Spirit to me so that I can know You more fully and love You more dearly. Change me into a new person who wants to glorify You in all I do. In Jesus' name, amen.

If you are already a believer (Praise God!), has this day's study encouraged you to break the chains of sin the world keeps trying to wrap you in? What is your key takeaway from today's study?

Pray:

Lord God Almighty, help me to feed my heart, mind and soul with Your Word instead of this world. Strengthen my resolve to spend time in prayer. Give me a heart that longs to know You more fully. Take away my worldly desires and help me to be honest concerning my sin. Give me joy and thankfulness in all circumstances. Amen.

THE TRUTH ABOUT LOVE IN PRACTICE

- Make a list of all the things you are thankful for. When you are upset or hurting read the list. Joy is rooted in thankfulness. Kindness is rooted in thankfulness. Adopt an attitude of gratitude.
- Before you go to sleep at night think about one kind thing you did for someone else that day.
- Listen to praise music when you are doing mundane tasks.
- Based on your gifts, volunteer one day a month (at least) at a local ministry.
- Pray to start your day and to end your day. *(You can follow the PRAY model: P= Praise Him. R = Repent. Be specific and honest about your sin. A = Ask. Lay your requests/burdens at His feet. Y = Yield to God's Will.)*

Day Five - Discussion Questions

Have you ever considered how there are different kinds of love? Do you now have a better understanding of how God's Agape love is supernatural, and why we can say, God is love?

Can you see how having a strong relationship with Christ is essential to having healthy relationships with others? What are some relationship challenges you've faced?

What are some of the things you will look for in a future spouse? Is marrying a believer important to you? Why or why not?

What are some practical ways you can live your life as an image bearer of Christ in this dark world?

How do we live amid all of this darkness, pain, and suffering? Why do believers have a reason to be thankful and joyful even in the darkness?

About the Author

Stephanie Cardel is the founder of Lighthouse Literary Agency. She lives on a farm in middle Tennessee with her husband and their goldendoodle. They have three grown children and five precious grandchildren.

She led VBS and wrote and directed Christmas plays at her church when her children were young. Then she turned to the women's ministry and was active planning events and leading Bible studies, which she continues to do. She had the pleasure of being on the crew of three faith-based films and a Christmas movie and even had a small part in three of them.

She taught abstinence-based sex education in the public schools for five years. She co-wrote a Christian advice column on the *Daughter of Delight* website for two years, which is still available in the archives. She is a member of the MidSouth SCBWI and the ACFW.

This Isn't Shakespeare is her debut novel.

Connect with Stephanie online at:
www.stephaniecardel.com

Also Available From

WordCrafts Press

Learning as I Go
by Christy Bass Adams

In the Boat with Jesus
by Marian Rizzo

God in the Commonplace
by Beverly Clopton

Illuminations
by Paula K. Parker

When the Other Boot Drops
by Jeff Keene II

The Gift of Peace
by Kira Marie McCullough & Keb Burns

www.wordcrafts.net

Made in the USA
Monee, IL
24 November 2025